Wisdom Tales in an imprint of World Wisdom, Inc.

Library of Congress Cataloging-in-Publication Data

Names: Demi, author.
Title: Gifts of our Lady of Guadalupe : patroness of Latin America / by Demi.
Description: Bloomington, IN : Wisdom Tales, 2018. |
Identifiers: LCCN 2017045609 (print) | LCCN 2017046183 (ebook) | ISBN
9781937786748 (epub) | ISBN 9781937786731 (casebound : alk. paper)
Subjects: LCSH: Guadalupe, Our Lady of--History--Juvenile literature.
Classification: LCC BT660.G8 (ebook) | LCC BT660.G8 D425 2018 (print) | DDC
232.91/7097253--dc23
LC record available at https://url.emailprotection.link/?aQIGj4lOvUgMGIEdjJ2U_yA8YxILGM-
DU42yXJJqiuEG0~

Printed in China on acid-free paper.
Production Date: January 2018
Plant & Location: Printed through Asia Pacific Offset
Job/Batch#: Q17120242

For information address Wisdom Tales,
P.O. Box 2682, Bloomington, Indiana, 47402-2682
www.wisdomtalespress.com

# Gifts of
# Our Lady of Guadalupe

## Patroness of Latin America
## DEMI

In 1519 A.D., the powerful Spanish conquistador, Hernan Cortes, landed in Mexico. Within two years he conquered the great Aztec Empire in Mexico City.

Cortes then destroyed the Aztec temples and
built Catholic churches in their place.

He sent Franciscan monks to convert the people, but because the Spaniards were so brutal, few Aztecs joined.

After twelve years, one Indian farmer named Juan Diego
felt the great need to pray, and so he joined the
Catholic parish in Mexico City.

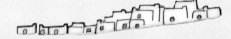

Just before dawn on Saturday the 9th
of December, 1531, Juan Diego was on his way
to Mass. He came to a hill known as Tepeyac just as day broke.

H e could hear the
singing of many
beautiful birds, and when the birds
stopped singing, the whole hill seemed
to sing in response to them. Juan Diego
thought he must be dreaming, and asked himself,
"Is this the place where Heaven comes to earth?"

Suddently the singing stopped. As he looked towards the top of the hill he heard someone calling his name. Then he was amazed to see a most beautiful, radiant, and splendid lady.

Her clothes glimmered like the sun and her brilliance
made the rocks and plants sparkle like jewels.
Where she stood, rays of light shone like a rainbow.

Juan Diego bowed deeply before her, as she told him that she was Holy Mary, the Mother of God. Then she instructed him to go to the bishop in Mexico City and ask him to build a great church so that people would come to know her love, compassion, and protection.

J uan Diego went to Bishop Juan de Zumárraga in Mexico City. But the bishop did not believe his fantastic story. Sadly, Juan Diego went back to the hill of Tepeyac where the beautiful lady was waiting for him. He told her that the bishop had not listened and asked her to send someone else, for he was merely a humble farmer. "I have chosen you," she answered. "Go back to the bishop. Tell him again to build a church in the name of Holy Mary, Mother of God, who has sent you!"

Juan Diego again went to the bishop with the message of the beautiful lady. He described everything he had seen, heard, and experienced. The bishop listened, but he said he needed a sign, some proof of her actual existence.

Juan Diego hurried back to the beautiful lady with the bishop's request. She said, "That is fine. Return here tomorrow for the sign he asked for."

But the next day Juan Diego's uncle was very sick. So Juan Diego went out to find a doctor and priest for him. As he was passing by Tepeyac hill the beautiful lady suddenly appeared. "Do not worry," she said. "Am I not your mother? Rest assured, your uncle is already cured and well."

Then she asked Juan to climb the hill and gather flowers for her. It was a bitterly cold day in December where not even a blade of grass could possibly grow. But when Juan Diego climbed to the top of the hill he was amazed to see thousands of Castilian roses bursting into bloom.

Joyously Juan Diego picked many flowers and brought them back to the beautiful lady. She took the flowers and put them carefully into his cape.

"My dear son," she said. "These beautiful roses are my proof for the bishop. Tell him everything you saw, heard, and experienced. Inspire the bishop, so that my church will be built at once."

Juan Diego went straightaway to the bishop's residence. When he entered the bishop's room, Juan Diego opened his cloak and all the beautiful roses fell to the floor. Roses in December! Here was the proof the bishop had asked for. But there was even more proof, for imprinted in dazzling colors on Juan Diego's white cloak was a full-size image of Mary, the Holy Mother of God! The bishop and all the priests fell to their knees in worship.

T he bishop prayed and begged forgiveness for not honoring her request. He said to Juan Diego, "Now show us where the lady from Heaven wishes her church to be built!"

And Juan Diego led them to the place on the hill of Tepeyac. Then the bishop invited everyone to come and help build her church.

The bishop had the holy image of Mary hung in the new church so all the people could see and admire it. Then the whole city came to see her precious image and pray before it. They marveled at the miraculous way it had appeared, since absolutely no one on earth could have painted such a beautiful and indestructible image.

The image of Our Lady of Guadalupe was so powerful that ten million Aztecs converted to Catholicism in just eight years' time.

In 1754, when Pope Benedict XIV saw her image, he fell to his knees and declared, "To no other nation has this been done!"

In 1910, Pope Pius X first proclaimed her as the Celestial Patroness of Latin America.

Today the image of Our Lady of Guadalupe hangs in the Basilica of Our Lady of Guadalupe in Mexico City. It is the most popular Marian shrine in all the world, attracting millions of pilgrims every year. And the miracles of Guadalupe continue to this day.

# About the Virgin of Guadalupe

The "beautiful lady" who appeared to Juan Diego is called by various names; two of the most common are the Virgin of Guadalupe (in Spanish, La Virgen de Guadalupe) and Our Lady of Guadalupe (in Spanish, Nuestra Señora de Guadalupe). In Spanish she is also called La Virgen Morena or the Brown Virgin.

Over the centuries, she has received many formal or informal titles, including "Patroness of New Spain" (by Pope Benedict XIV in 1754), "Patroness of Latin America" (by Pope Pius X in 1910), and "Queen of Mexico and Empress of the Americas" (by Pope Pius XII in 1945).

The basilica dedicated to the Virgin of Guadalupe receives about 20 million pilgrims per year, making it the most popular Christian pilgrimage site in the world.

The Hill of Tepeyac, where the Virgin first appeared, later became part of the town of Guadalupe. The town of Guadalupe is today considered a suburb of Mexico City.

The Virgin of Guadalupe spoke to Juan Diego in his native language called Nahuatl (the language of the Aztec Empire). In her appearance, she was also like a native woman. Partly for this reason, she has been loved by many native people of the Americas.

In the image, Mary is "clothed with the sun" and with "the moon at her feet," as described in Revelation 12:1.

According to some, the stars that appear on the image appear to be astronomically correct, corresponding to how the constellations would have looked in the winter sky on December 12, 1531.

Some observers have noted that the Virgin's eyes, when examined through a microscope, reflect the images of the witnesses present at its unveiling, including Juan Diego and the bishop.

In Mexico millions of women and men are named Guadalupe (or "Lupe" for short), in honor of the apparition of the Virgin of Guadalupe.

December 12 is the feast day commemorating the apparation of Our Lady of Guadalupe.